108 Divinel

Spiritual Poetry
A Disciple's Journey

By

Jasdeep Hari Bhajan Singh Khalsa
Onkardeep Singh Khalsa

Spiritual Poetry: A Disciple's Journey

By   Jasdeep Hari Bhajan Singh Khalsa
      Onkardeep Singh Khalsa

ISBN 978-1-4092-8893-0
Published by Lulu, Inc: www.lulu.com

Cover design by Dipali Haria: www.dipsydesigns.co.uk
Reviewed by: BSB Publishers

Contact Us
To contact us please email: info@spiritualpoetry.co.uk
For upcoming books please visit: www.spiritualpoetry.co.uk

Dedicated to:
Mr. and Mrs. Bhatia, Our Beloved Parents

We must not hope to be mowers,
And to gather the ripe old ears,
Unless we have first been sowers,
And watered the furrows with tears,
It is not just as we take it,
This mystical world of ours,
Life's field will yield as we make it,
A harvest of thorns or of flowers.

- Johann Wolfgang von Goethe

Introduction

First and foremost we would like to thank God for allowing us to express ourselves in this form, and also thank you for allowing us to share this poetry with you. We have written these poems as a tool to expand your awareness and give you an insight into our individual experience of Reality. We have not written anything that is not true to us or which we do not practice ourselves, there is therefore an authenticity to these poems.

The intention behind these poems is not to dictate to you what is right or wrong, but instead, to act as an inspiration for you on your spiritual journey. These poems are our mind, heart and soul blended together into the eloquence of language and are not meant to offend you in any way.

If even an iota of a poem touches your heart, then our job is complete because it is our continued prayer that everyone should be healthy, happy and holy in their lives. So, if you are touched in some way by this poetry, then we would kindly request that you share these poems with someone else, and help touch another heart.

Blessings,

Jasdeep & Onkardeep.

Contents

A Day Of Freedom

Today is a day of freedom,
Today is a day of martyrdom,
Freedom from time and space,
Martyrdom of life and breath.

Oh mortal, when will you pull through?
When will you fall out of negativity?
Oh mortal, when will kindness brew?
When will you turn to progressivity?

Today is a day of freedom,
Today is a day of martyrdom,
Freedom from time and space,
Martyrdom of life and breath.

Oh mortal, when will you pray to be free?
When will you shine like the Sun?
Oh mortal, when will God's destiny you lead?
When will you turn to the Infinite One?

Today is a day of freedom,
Today is a day of martyrdom,
Freedom from time and space,
Martyrdom of life and breath.

A Life Worth Living

Consciousness.
The access to freedom,
Reality is a paradox,
Infinity equal to one,
Mind filled with blocks.

Purpose.
The search for meaning,
Muddled in a story,
Of what is happening,
Engrossed in a false fury.

Intelligence.
How can we understand,
A logic beyond logic,
Unravelling strand by strand,
Becoming a walking stick.

Wisdom.
To know the unknown,
Language is so limited,
A path is shown,
Freedom no longer inhibited.

Experience.
The source of wisdom,
A life worth living,
No shadow of doubt,
A life of giving.

Life.
Living to higher consciousness,
Serving through the heart,
Every day a new freshness,
Every day is the start.

A Place In My Mind

A place in my mind,
Stiller than stillness,
A place I want to find,
The cure to my illness.

Pleasure gives no satisfaction,
It's just creation's distraction,
Joy gives me attraction,
It's my natural reaction.

A space in my heart,
A void that can't be seen,
Like a blank canvas of art,
Painting it my life's dream.

Love allows you to see,
Flowing through mankind,
Setting your mind free,
Spreading a light so kind.

A gap in my soul,
The flower needs to flower,
A part of the whole,
No more illusion of power.

Humility makes me complete,
I'm everything without anything,
Falling at Guru's lotus feet,
I'm something with nothing.

A place in my mind,
A place I have found,
The cure to being blind,
Where love is all around.

A Prayer to Waheguru (Wonderful God)

Waheguru, Waheguru I chant to the world,
But no one listens, no one has heard,
I am in a despondent situation, one which is hard on me,
Yet no one will help to set my situation free.

Waheguru, Waheguru I chant a prayer to you,
What should I do?
No one cares; no one dares help me, except for you.

I walk astray towards the light,
To find a way to give me sight,
And to free my situation.

On my return, I found the supreme light,
And my troubles changed from wrong to right,
For this Waheguru I thank you with all my might.

And so Waheguru, Waheguru, this prayer I bellow to you,
Keep everyone safe and keep me safe too,
Because the bright day can become a dark night,
And fears can rise up to a fight,
Waheguru, show these people right,
To your great Kingdom of Light.

A Rhyme and Rhythm

A rhyme and rhythm so central in life, in every situation a consistency rife, some seek the chaos, others find a pattern. But what is the aim of doing the same? Or the benefit of consistent inconsistency? The behaviours of many based on others. An animal world, evolution? Three things rule the animal mind. Thoughts of food, sex, shelter to survive. What are we, true to ourselves? How many humans are human in themselves? A question so basic, its answer concerning. Who will lead the change; you and me. Raise up, rise up, do not accept the quo. You and me, let us be the future now. Let us think and create what we wish to see, for that is in the end what shall be.

Create a rhyme, a rhythm so true. Your frequency shall match the universal Guru. Vibrate and chant this beautiful music, blissful bliss so shall it be, the mind dances to the souls tune. Generate, Operate, Destroy, utilise this boon. Light up, light down, wear your God given crown. Become the rhyme and the rhythm. Rhythm and the rhyme. How sublime, oh how sublime, oh how sublime my divine.

All Walks Of Life

Human is always infinite,
Finite is our mind,
Bonded to our thoughts,
Taught to be blind.

Every single being,
Seeing something unique,
Seek to have freedom,
Wisdom and physique.

All walks of life,
Rife is the insanity,
Vanity we just crave,
Brave have some sanity.

Beauty in everyone,
Begun has the New-Age,
Sage in every soul,
Goal is escaping rage.

Humanity a collective body,
Everybody seeks a connection,
Rejection and hate rule,
Dual is our perception.

Perfection does not exist,
Persist in accepting,
Loving each personality,
Duality is now leaving.

Human is always infinite,
Finite is our mind,
Bonded to our thoughts,
Learning to be kind.

An Evening Prayer

Please bless me with the Naam, Your Name, so that I may remember you night and day, forever.
Please bless me with the power to serve others with humility and compassion.
Please bless me with the discipline of a soldier, to rise in the Amrit Veylah, the hours before dawn, to not only wake up but to get up and stay up, so that I may sing Your Glorious Praises,
And the fearlessness to be victorious in every facet of life in Your Name.
My Lord, please bless me with the Blessed Vision of Your Darshan, Your Presence, which I have longed for so many lifetimes.

To you my Lord, I offer my mind, body and soul.
To you my Lord, I'm forever a sacrifice at your feet.

I thank you for such a beautiful day and please protect me at night. Sat Naam.

Battle Experience

Fighting a battle using strength and wit,
What one gains is more than just a rush,
Get a hit and the light becomes lit,
Looking, everything seems so lush.

Get going from the start of the day,
Whatever one does tomorrow,
Keep in mind the fight at bay,
Many get lost in simple sorrow.

Life provides many situations,
What one can learn from them is always new,
Life provides many sensations,
The love of the Lord, experienced by the few.

Be Empowered

We must be empowered,
And empower all,
Empower every limb,
So we never fall.

Create a spiritual wall,
Aura must be strong,
Power comes from God,
By singing God's song.

Go beyond right or wrong,
Turn every cell into light,
Become a real human being,
Inner battle we fight.

Power is in spiritual might,
No greater strength is known,
Power is in prayer with love,
No greater path has shown.

We must be empowered,
And empower all,
Empower every limb,
So we never fall.

Up and down part of life,
Spirit brings you through,
Learn from every experience,
God's laws always true.

Don't let anger brew,
Reap what we sow,
Make mind the arrow,
Make heart the bow.

No one high or low,
Everyone just the same,
No one good or bad,
Individuals we remain.

We must be empowered,
And empower all,
Empower every limb,
So we never fall.

Love is the game,
Bliss our birth right,
Fearlessness the effect,
Spirituality our height.

Guru our blessed sight,
Giver of liberation,
Be dead whilst alive,
Humility is elevation.

Have truth in action,
Serve God in everyone,
All action has reaction,
God is always One.

We must be empowered,
And empower all,
Empower every limb,
So we never fall.

Be Free

Be who you really are, be to be,
Excel in your thoughts, excel.

Feed your mind with all that you are,
Remember, remember, remember shall you.
Excel in your thought, excel,
Expand yourself beyond, propel.

Be you, be me, be free.

befree

Be Who You Really Are

Mighty people we are on this world,
Look at my strength,
Look at my wealth,
Look at my health I say to you.

Is this not what life is? This life we live,
Why a con? Why so unfree?
I ask you why do you live?
What is the purpose of the world I am within?
I say none, there is nothing, live as you wish, it is something.

What of greatness and higher living?
What of care, respect, a life worth living?
I say to you there is nothing, only a complex organism,
Nothing greater, a kind of shapeless mirror.
Why do people seek for more? Life is life, live it, nothing more.

Now I say these things, what do you feel?
I say you know not you, or of what is real.
I say what you say for what you are is me.
What then becomes of that nothing? Feel.

If the biggest joke is that your life is a game,
What good then comes from searching in vain?
Is not the aim to live life, fame, no pain?
Let me say, you have found the game.

The game we play not to win,
In all other endeavours we seek victory,
But for this journey we see not the end,
I say it is a shame, even though win we shall my friend.

So why set out to remember what we know?
Is it useful to move, think, dance to and fro?
It is surely not the aim to let life pass but what do we learn in the life
class?
Good, bad, heaven hell, right wrong, jail cell, rubbish.

The aim is to Be Who You Really Are,
A myriad of choices, decisions made afar,

Seek to be Truth for it shall set you free,
A life worth living, for you and for me!

To become nothing is to fall to the ground,
Find the roots and turn them upside down,
Open your mind to that which you are not,
For through this awareness you shall find that which you are, your
full lot.

That which you are is infinitely big,
No person, country, world can capture your glory,
In this universe we live to Be,
Ultimately you are everything, including me.

Through this awareness, a higher cause can be found,
For that which is for me, serves all and the ground,
Live not for winning but serve yourself,
Through this service you shall find peace,
God bless, God bless, God bless.

Becoming

You must become the change you wish to see,
You must become the light of purity,
You must become the soldier and the saint,
You must become the vision for the faint.

That is your destiny,
That is your velocity,
That is your capacity,
That is your surety.

You must become the balance of earth and sky,
You must become the habit of learn and try,
You must become the beam of everlasting light,
You must become the stream of unified might.

That is your way,
That is your path,
That is your day,
That is your bath.

Being Beautiful

One should be beautiful without insecurity,
and radiant without deception,
One should be kind without hostility,
and truthful without exception.

One should be accepting without division,
and peaceful without mentality,
One should be perfect without flaw,
and decisive without duality.

One should be loving with heart,
and infinite with Infinity,
One should be bright with awareness,
and balanced with neutrality.

Children Of Light

Children of light and beauty,
Search your might and duty,
Children of excellence and peace,
Find your success and release.

Children of life and purity,
Surpass your strife and mutiny,
Children of love and health,
Share your joy and wealth.

Children of heaven and earth,
Create your haven and worth,
Children of grace and courage,
Grow your faith and flourish.

Children of focus and power,
Become a lotus and flower,
Children of truth and meditation,
Stay in youth and salvation.

Constant Flight

Life a mysterious veil and misty maze masking a great battle of the mind,
Hazy, the souls wander following the hedonistic signs blind.

The surroundings manifest flourishing flowers, a garden of bliss,
Souls wondering with precise aim in this great life, but they miss!

The target misjudged, the battle left hidden, the journey taken to find the end so long,
But, it's not where you finish, it's where you begin...Ong!

Daily Meditation

Walking up the road, a summers morning,
The birds chirping, railway blurping,
A red helicopter soars overhead,
Man walks, no troubles left ahead.

A light breeze cools the face,
The sun's rays kiss me, relax, no haste.
Where are you going? When do u stay?
Life of questions, pray pray pray.

Colour, washed, mixed made all around,
Sounds bristle and whoosh, heard, not found,
Smell busy, sharp, unclear washed,
Senses engaged, awareness the cost.

The yellow line marks the limit,
Beyond exists but dangerous is it called,
Be careful, limits safe, do not fall!
The train arrives, this is the call!

A busy rush of senses explode,
Information load on load,
Smiles, eyes closed, dance to the beat,
What a variety oh Divine, innumerable feet.

The world passes, so quick we go,
I am wonderstruck, the days begun behold!
Life so diverse, so vast, beeeeeeeep!
Wander, eat, sleep, a human life or sheep?

Silent meditation, silent it becomes,
Do not offend, scare, silent hums,
Advertise to the live, give more need more,
A consumer filled world, what a bore!

I am you, you are me, extend and expand,
Whether you sit, hope, wish or stand,
Tired, aloft, the soul wishes to travel,
Without you my Divine, all is lost! Unravel.

Look but do not touch, life's unwritten,
Magnificent, lovely, mind bitten,
Stop go stop go, the journey continues,
Journey coordinated by a voice hidden.

The darkness approaches so quickly it seems,
Lost I would be, without the inner light lit,
Journey goes on, no fear dear,
You are guided by the tracks, light shall reappear.

The journey's end I know I will achieve,
My state, my being is what matters before I leave,
Life is the journey, no matter the end,
The end is guaranteed, my divine friend.

Daughter of Guru Gobind Singh

Daughter of Guru Gobind Singh,
Deathless Father of all,
Stay beautiful, bountiful and blissful,
Stand confident and walk tall.

Stay heart centred and humble,
Stay humorous and kind,
Never will you again stumble,
Everything in Guru we find.

Daughter of Guru Gobind Singh,
Deathless Father of humanity,
Stay beautiful, bountiful and blissful,
The world is in insanity.

Never have worry or sorrow,
Gifts the Guru will send,
Either today or tomorrow,
It'll be alright in the end.

Daughter of Guru Gobind Singh,
Deathless Father of everyone,
Stay beautiful, bountiful and blissful,
Life's essence you have won.

Always be you,
Everything is on the mend,
Bliss is with the Guru,
No need to ever pretend.

Daughter of Guru Gobind Singh,
Deathless Father of mankind,
Stay beautiful, bountiful and blissful,
Stay perfect in heart and mind.

Your destiny is set in stone,
The road ahead is clear,
Never will you be alone,
No need for anxiety or fear.

Daughter of Guru Gobind Singh,
Deathless Father of all,
Stay beautiful, bountiful and blissful,
Stand confident and walk tall.

Dearest Mother Earth

Dearest Mother Earth,
The Mother of mankind,
Through death and birth,
Her care we find.

But man isn't kind,
To Her at all,
Destruction we shall find,
And man shall fall.

Man must change his ways,
Before it's too late,
Heal Her and pray,
Man must change his fate.

Mother Earth heals us,
Provides all we need,
No need to fuss,
Just do this deed.

Mother loves her child,
Mother provides everything,
Child has gone wild,
Chaos the child brings.

Trees are so healing,
Water is so quenching,
Flowers are so calming,
Air is so cleansing.

When will we realise,
These resources are critical,
Without them we're paralysed,
Stop being so political.

Polluting her we'll die,
Strangling our own neck,
This is no lie,
Humans are a speck.

Compared to the universe,
We're so very small,
Yet we're so perverse,
We like to stand tall.

Pretending we own land,
Doing what we please,
With every single strand,
We are Her disease.

But still Mother loves,
Giving is Her nature,
Time to rise above,
Time to now mature.

Earth we must heal,
Treading the Earth gently,
Earth we must feel,
Treating the Earth gratefully.

Keep Her in your prayers,
Love Her in your way,
Show Her all your care,
Then She'll be okay.

By taking responsibility,
Humans will cause a shift,
Reducing the probability,
That from peace we drift.

Tomorrow is too late,
Today we must change,
No need to wait,
Caring is not strange.

Her care we find,
Through death and birth,
The Mother of mankind,
Dearest Mother Earth.

Desire And Wishes

Without the True Guru, my mind continually wanders.
Without the Grace of God, I am continually plundered.
Desire has seized me by the throat.
Maya has broken my only escape boat.

My heart longs for that permanent love of God, night and day.
My mind wishes to see God shining everywhere, in every way.
Without the Grace of God, I am continually plundered.
Without the True Guru, my mind continually wanders.

Destiny

Freewill to choose?
Destiny a ruse?
Only one thing to do,
Submit to The True Guru.

We are the dust of the puppets,
The highest He sits.
Parading around like we know,
Everything just for show.

Whatever The King wills,
The creation fulfils.
We don't know we know,
We are the lowest of the low.

Karma takes us near or far,
Previous actions set the par.
Our destiny we can change.
But for some this seems strange.

Freewill to choose?
Destiny a ruse?
Only one thing to do,
Submit to The True Guru.

Direction Infinity

The world follows many,
Great masters are some,
Some follow any,
Directionless they become.

Living life is lost,
The meaning burnt,
Karma takes the cost,
Lessons remain unlearnt.

The pursuit of things,
An illusion store,
Puppets on strings,
Less freedom is more.

Follow the true mark,
Then one will win,
Most search in dark,
But Truth lies within.

Love is the focus,
Concentrated divinity,
Flourishing lotus,
Direction infinity.

Enlightenment

Enlightenment.
A series of realisations,
Making you lighter,
Lighter and lighter.

Fulfilment.
Being fully-filled,
With love,
Love and love.

Courage.
Being courageous,
Every moment,
Moment and moment.

Royal Radiance.
Seeing beauty,
In everyone,
Everyone and everyone.

Even If

Even if you built a thousand castles,
With their walls reinforced with steel,
And put in each castle, a thousand guards,
Still you are not protected from the fire of desire.

Even if you had eternal wealth,
With factories and endless property,
And each building with endless furniture,
Still you cannot buy protection from the fire of desire.

Even if you did millions of acts of charity,
With selfless service without reward,
And meditation day and night on the Supreme,
Still you are not granted protection from the fire of desire.

The fire of desire can only be defeated with love,
One can have power, money and even a good heart,
But until the mind merges with the Infinite, all is useless,
Learning to love the creation is the best education,
Meditation and selfless service alone is useless,
But if it is done with love, then desire is shattered eternally.

Ever So Many

Ever so many people,
Ever so many voices,
Ever so many ways,
Increasing day by day.

Ever so many people,
My voice so small,
How will God hear?
Progression at a wall.

Ever so many ways,
Path ahead not clear,
Time again I pray,
Take my confusion away.

Progress in God's hands,
God hears us all,
Inner knower of hearts,
Stand confident and tall.

Listen and search deep,
The answer always there,
Choose God ever moment,
Divine laws always fair.

Follow the voice within,
Path must be love,
Reap what we sow,
Free as a dove.

Ever so many people,
Ever so many voices,
Ever so many ways,
Increasing day by day.

Everyday Is a Miracle

Everyday is a miracle,
Even if you don't realise,
It's a privilege to be alive,
Even if you don't contemplate.

Everyday is a miracle,
Vegetables growing from Earth,
Birds chirping in the sky,
Trees standing tall and strong.

Everyday is a miracle,
Sun lights up everything,
Rain cools everyone down,
The weather is dancing.

Everyday is a miracle,
People have so much energy,
Everyone rushing and doing,
Trying to progress through life.

Everyday is a miracle,
The day is for working,
The night for some rest,
The flux is so perfect.

Everyday is a miracle,
Lush colours light up everything,
But to think we're just a speck,
In the universe so infinite.

Everyday is a miracle,
Every moment is so precious,
Tomorrow anything could happen,
Why not live for today?

Everyday is a miracle,
Even if you don't realise,
It's a privilege to be alive,
Even if you don't contemplate.

Everything Is You

Every being is You. Every body is You.
Every creature is You. Every soul is You.
Every animal is You. Every fish is You.
Every bird is You. Every insect is You.

Every atom is You. Every particle is You.
Every cell is You. Every fragment is You.
Everything is You, yet I still cannot see You?
This is a tragedy, it is the tragedy of all tragedy.

Oh God, the mind cannot help but ponder Your power,
Upon Your creation Your blessings constantly shower.
Oh God, what power do us mortals have, to flower,
I beg for the grace from the True Guru, to empower.

Oh God, there is no one else worth begging before,
Day and night I am knocking at Your door.
Oh God, shower Your mercy on Your servant so poor,
Begging for your grace, this is the perfect chore.

Every mountain is You. Every ocean is You.
Every stone is You. Every raindrop is You.
Every field is You. Every rainbow is You.
Every grain is You. Every colour is You.

Every flower is You. Every tree is You.
Every petal is You. Every leaf is You.
Everything is You, yet I still feel separated from You?
The heart is in turmoil, it is the turmoil of all turmoil.

Oh God, grant me a moment of Your radiant light,
So that I may never be separated from Your sight.
Oh God, the jewel of my forehead is in night,
I beg for the Naam, the vibration of Your might.

Oh God, the five thieves rob me continually everyday,
The account of karma is now bankrupt and in decay.
Oh God, without You what good does my life display,
Bless me a moment of Your love, this is what I pray.

Family Love

Love in the family,
Love for The Lord,
Harder it becomes,
Nothing is assured.

Easier to lose focus,
Easier to lose sight,
Balance must be struck,
The soul reaps its luck.

Love is the key,
Attachment the devil,
Family brings you closer,
Serving sets you free.

Love the family,
Love The Lord,
Easier it becomes,
Everything is assured.

Finding The One

Finding the one,
To make me whole,
The quest has begun,
This is my life's goal.

Haystacks are too much of a pun,
It's more like a bullet without a gun,
You run, and find no one,
The art of life remains undone.

I've searched the mountains,
I've searched the stars,
I've searched the fountains,
I've searched near and far.

Running into the forest,
To find some joy inside,
The mind still at unrest,
There's too much pride.

My soul is waiting,
It needs relating,
God keeps loving,
No need for hating.

The one was there all along,
The answer so simple and clear,
The universe singing a song,
It's something I feel and hear.

I've found infinity.
I've found the gun.
I've found divinity.
I've found the one.

Forgotten They Are Not

Today we stand free,
A priceless debt we owe,
Together you and me,
Let the blessings grow.

Bless us with peace,
May we drop our enmity,
Our ego's we release,
Help us see our unity.

Bless us with courage,
Let us uphold what is right,
This life is a stage,
Help us shine bright.

Bless us with fortitude,
May we do well even in strain,
In this life, not so crude,
Help us overcome any pain

Bless us with Your love,
With it our souls radiate,
Providing warmth like a glove,
Compassion becomes a trait.

Bless us with Your light,
And those who fought,
Provide us with the might,
So life's victory can be sought.

Those brave souls,
Fallen as the enemy shot,
Fighting for other's goals,
Forgotten they are not.

Vaheguru Ji Ka Khalsa
Vaheguru Ji Ke Fateh

From Where Do The Rainbows Shine?

From where do the rainbows shine,
Is there a source to the beauty,
What makes bright people's eyes?
At night my soul cries,
For the Beloved within,
There is no sin,
Only that which brings one closer,
And takes one further away,
In the day, my soul sighs,
It wants complete merger,
Partial is not enough,
For when there is true merger,
There is no separation again,
When Oh Lord, when?
Will I see thy Lotus Feet,
When Oh Lord, when?
Will thy Saints I meet.
Day and night, night and day,
For Your Blessed Vision I pray,
Night and day, day and night,
I long for your sight.
From where do the rainbows shine,
Is there a source to the beauty?
What makes people's eyes bright?
Living for your service and duty.

God Bless

God bless everyone,
God bless the religion and race,
God bless the lost and won,
God bless the time and space.

God bless the rich and poor,
God bless the living and dying,
God bless the innocent and mature,
God bless the laughing and crying.

God bless the good and bad,
God bless the soldier and saint,
God bless the happy and sad,
God bless the strong and faint.

God bless the hungry and fed,
God bless the healthy and ill,
God bless the alive and dead,
God bless the disturbed and still.

God bless the tainted and pure,
God bless the bright and dim,
God bless the doubtful and sure,
God bless the light and grim.

God bless the sky and sea,
God bless the heaven and earth,
God bless the locked and free,
God bless the death and birth.

God bless the pen and sword,
God bless the silence and tune,
God bless the quiet and chord,
God bless the sun and moon.

God bless the time and space,
God bless the lost and won,
God bless the religion and race,
God bless everyone.

Hatred Flows

They are born in hate,
They grow up in hate,
They get married in hate,
They die in hate.

They are taught only hate,
They treat others with hate,
They speak words of hate,
They listen with hate.

Their friends are full of hate,
Their food is polluted with hate,
Their clothes stained with hate,
They sleep with hearts of hate.

They recite their prayers with hate,
They do their pilgrimages in hate,
They make their fasts in hate,
They perform their rituals in hate.

Their intellect is deluded with hate,
Their mind is filled with hate,
Their thoughts flow only with hate,
So how then can the love of God flow through their heart?

Only by meditating on the one God,
Only by recognising humanity as one,
Only by serving humanity as one,
Can the heart be pierced with the love of the One God.

Heritage of India

Heritage so far away,
Yet close to my heart,
A journey to the east,
Beauty in every part.

The sound of the Dhol,
An instrument with beat,
Bright colours everywhere,
Everyone touching feet.

The streets so noisy,
Always heat and floods,
Both affluence and poverty,
Huts made from mud.

Many saints and yogis,
Many wise honest men,
Many people of faith,
Many swords and pens.

Many imposters and thieves,
Many foolish lying souls,
Many people of darkness,
Many without a goal.

United by a flag,
A country of many divides,
Divided by a history,
A country of many lives.

I Am You

I am You,
God is my light,
Spirit gives me sight,
I am You.

I am a Learner,
Truth is my way,
To serve I pray,
I am a Learner.

I am a Seeker,
Consciousness is my reason,
Meditating all four seasons,
I am a Seeker.

I am a Yogi,
Union is my goal,
From part to whole,
I am a Yogi.

I am a Void,
God is my Father,
Earth the great Mother,
I am a Void.

I am a Servant,
Humility is my tool,
The Soul must rule,
I am a Servant.

I am a Lover,
Love is my life,
No enemy or strife,
I am a Lover.

I am You,
God is my light,
Spirit gives me sight,
I am You.

I Pray To Thee

I salute Thee, who let me live,
I salute Thee, who taught me to forgive,
I salute Thee, who kept me straight,
On the path to realise I'm great.

I bow to Thee, who gave me all,
I bow to Thee, who made me tall,
I bow to Thee, who showed me light,
On the path to reach my height.

I praise Thee, who set me free,
I praise Thee, who let me see,
I praise Thee, who is always there,
On the path to serve and share.

I serve Thee, who gave me awareness,
I serve Thee, who showed me fairness,
I serve Thee, who serves everyone,
On the path You Yourself begun.

I beg to Thee, every day I breathe,
My side you never leave,
I beg to Thee, great King of creations,
Please remove my worldly fascinations.

I pray to Thee, I pray to see,
A moment of your eternal beauty,
I pray to Thee, oh Creator of me,
May I be lost and merge in Thee.

I meditate upon Thee, to quieten my mind,
No greater love I shall find,
I meditate upon Thee, to give me focus,
My mind is like the locust.

I sacrifice to Thee, everything I own,
So I do not remain, it's just you alone,
I sacrifice to Thee, mind, body and soul,
By your grace, I'm complete and whole.

I've Searched All The Seven Seas

I've searched all the seven seas,
Only to find the eternal sea within,
I've searched all places of pilgrimage,
Only to find the shrine in my heart.

When my heart is ablaze with love,
How can I describe my state?
When my heart is overflowing with compassion,
Who can describe my state?

Tongue-tied and mesmerised,
I yearn for my Beloved Lord,
Spellbound and mystified,
I've become lost in the cosmos.

I seek neither the heavens nor the hells,
Nor the angels nor the demons,
I seek neither the good nor the bad,
Nor the pleasure nor the pain.

For my Lord to me is everlasting,
Unchanging and overflowing,
The support of support itself,
My Lord to me is everything.

Who can measure my love?
What instrument can capture its value?
For a moment feels like eternity,
As I die in my Beloved.

My Lord, My Lord, My Lord Beloved,
Have mercy upon me,
For I am but an innocent child,
Lost in the park of life.

My Lord, My Lord, My Lord Companion,
I burn to see Thee,
For I am but a tiny creature,
Lost in all of eternity.

In The Beginning

In the beginning when the sun rose up,
The rays of light beamed down on perfection,
And many asked the question "why does the sun go down?"
Some took interest, others didn't and went into meditation.

In the second age the sky was a darker blue,
The light streaks were dimmed,
And many became selfish and lost their hearts of red,
Some stayed closer to the light that had been trimmed.

In the third age the scales of justice were quite uneven,
The light further fainted,
And less would see the light even,
Some became infatuated in religions and rules that they painted.

In this final and fourth age people are egoists,
The light is as dim as a candle in the wind,
But the scale is not touching the ground,
Everyone is deceived and fooled by the matrix,
But there are still few around, who are awake and humble.

The world must wake up to the reality,
And using but only love, not meditation,
Raise their energies to the crown,
Just like, in the beginning.

Infinite, Forever

Never ending, beginning forever,
Present future, past,
Experience, life's endeavour,
World finite, contrast.

Endless, countless,
Within, unfounded,
Wealthy fame, fruitless
Unlimited, unbounded.

Boundless, vast,
Tenth gate, accessible,
Attachments, surpassed,
Immeasurable, inestimable.

Everlasting, continual,
Sow seed, water the crop,
Loving love, perpetual,
Continuous, nonstop.

Constant, incessant,
Daily practice, unwilling,
Meditatively sit, chant,
Interminable, unremitting.

Permanent, Eternal,
Reality, life parade,
Cleanly focus, internal,
Innumerable, myriad.

Limitless, incalculable,
Materially happy, addicted,
Divine peace, Insurmountable,
Numerous, unrestricted.

Unrestrained, bottomless,
Knowledgeable, clever,
Spiritual experience, true success,
Infinite, Forever.

Inverse Is The Game Of Love

Each star in the sky shining,
With my consciousness, intertwining,
There is no I and them,
From the same source we stem.

Inverse is the game of love,
Cursed are those who look above,
Or below to the underworlds,
From outside cannot Truth unfurl.

Bliss, can no kingdom provide,
Hidden like the pearl, inside,
Neither King, Queen, rich nor poor,
Can open our inner sacred door.

For I've searched earths and skies,
To find only but rotten lies,
Men of honour, life and light,
Becoming slaves to wrong and right.

The inner river of wondrous joy,
Which even the Gods must enjoy,
Everlasting, immortal, always there,
Flowing within those that share.

Each man and woman must decree,
Bliss sits inside of me,
This is every human's birth-right,
Yet ego is the biggest fight.

For, there is no I and them,
From the same source we stem,
So, cursed are those who look above,
Inverse is the game of love.

It's Just You

I see someone choking,
And question 'Why?'
The man was poking
his nose into others businesses.

I see someone joking,
And question 'Why?'
The woman was boasting
to her friends and family.

I see someone angry,
And question 'Why?'
The person wasn't in Shangri-la
and needed more from the world.

I don't see these people anymore,
I don't know why,
It doesn't matter anymore,
It's all just a lie, before your deceiving eyes.

The world continues to tick to death,
ticking it is plundered,
no remembrance about the place of rest,
ticking it is blundered.

Such a weird place,
I don't understand,
I don't understand,
It's just You,
It's just You.

Just Like A Disease

We are just like a disease
infecting Mother Earth,
Like rats on the ship,
ambiguous to the damage we cause.

Just like as a foot stuck in the soil
becomes quickly infested with insects,
so are we humans spoiling
our world, with our own world.

Blindly we follow our Gods
of TV, gossip, fortune and fame,
Too engrossed with why, how and when,
Does this not seem lame?

We can only blame, ourselves, for the pain,
Since we write our own destinies
with every second that passes,
growing older and white haired we die in vain.

The meaning of life never known,
peace of mind never been shown
before your eyes, like drowning,
and never seeing the surface.

Stop frowning, it was you, who chose not to swim,
And see the True world of True beauty,
This was your birth right and duty
Loosing this vision, we stay in mind's mutiny.

Yet from being a disease, we have been shown the cure,
By submitting and loving we become One with the creator
of the creation, being so faithful and sure
that all is One, everywhere, always.

Without this understanding,
only brings more torture and pain,
Why can't we get this into our brain,
which is filled with ego and darkness?

We all pray,
that may, the light shine forth,
And light up the darkness,
Of the disease of the mind.

Keep Up

Work, sleep, eat, drink,
Laugh, dance, write, think,
Breathe, breathe, stop, breathe,
Up late, mind greed.

No focus, crystallise,
Sit still, meditation not tried,
Time now, used, hide,
Following pursuits, soul guide.

Easily done in this life of non-stop work,
Priorities set, soul left, murk.
Commitment spread,
Life's aims mind led.

Break the circle, break the habit,
Adapt, grow, navel lit.
Reassess, time set, commit,
In this life, time limit.

Keep up, keep up,
No guilt, no guilt,
Everything will come, will come
Reach you shall, you shall.

Keeping Up

Materialism is rife,
Following flocks of sheep,
There is no bliss of life,
Awake, we remain asleep.

Desires out of control,
Blocking out reality,
Trying to reach life's goal,
Filled with uncertainty.

Depression is flowing,
Seems no way out,
Life's vision going,
Mind is in doubt.

What do I do?
Where do I go?
Where is the clue?
How can peace flow?

Seeking Guru's guidance,
Guru dispelled the dark,
No more subsidence,
Guru is my shield and arc.

Vibration flows through,
Shabad has set me free,
Hope has been renewed,
Heart is in glee.

True congregation,
Has uplifted my being,
Renewed the motivation,
Mind is all freeing.

Breath has uplifted,
Blockage is no more,
Weight has been shifted,
Soul is at core.

Always keeping up,
When the going gets tough,
Always keeping up,
Takes you through the rough.

Keep in the Shabad,
Keep in true congregation,
Keep in the breath,
Find your destination.

Lake Of The Mind

Lake of the mind,
To which we're bound,
Thoughts creates ripples,
Can peace be found?

Lake is disturbed,
From countless lives,
Countless births, deaths,
Children and wives.

We are a drop,
God is the ocean,
How to become free,
From the grip of emotion?

To still the lake,
Needs grace and devotion,
The mind always creating,
Hate and commotion.

We need a Guru,
Guru is a wave,
Fully conscious and clear,
How ourselves to save?

We are waves too,
Not conscious of whole,
Everything organised,
All playing a role.

To play life's game,
Is to win infinity,
To lose all limits,
To freedom and ability.

This is only achieved,
When mind is still,
Heart can then shine,
With an inner will.

Life Is A Business

Life is a business,
With inflows and outflows,
With assets and liabilities,
With an account to show.

Let the inflow be love,
Grow it day-by-day,
Let the outflow be ego,
Don't let it stay.

Balance the accounts,
Sell the liabilities,
Build on the assets,
Of prayer and humility.

Everyone is in debt,
Debt is increasing everyday,
How can we win life?
And be blissful always?

To make a profit,
Loss must be recovered,
An excess amount remains,
Account is then accepted.

Daily meditation and prayer,
Reduces debt daily,
Every moment very sacred,
Life is won simply.

Each moment we're trading,
Through action and reaction,
Karmic law is universal,
Be careful every transaction.

Bliss is a birthright,
Shabad holds the key,
Consciousness fixed on Guru,
Heart is in glee.

Life Is But A Probability

Life is but a probability,
Death the only certainty,
What will we choose to be?
Ordinary or extraordinary?

Extraordinary isn't superhuman,
It's deciding that you can,
Even if you cannot,
It's deciding your life's plot.

By accepting yourself,
You'll realise your true-self,
For you are a King and Queen,
Of universes yet undreamed.

There'll be highs and lows,
Yet no one is high or low,
Each are as they are,
Each aren't as they aren't.

For life is lived diagonally,
Not vertically, nor horizontally,
Don't recite this mentally,
Instead live it practically.

Step out of your comfort zone,
And the path you'll be shown,
Have trust in the universe,
And gracious Mother Earth.

For commitment to a cause,
Will create only but miracles,
Leaving behind a legacy,
From eternity to eternity.

Even with all your limitations,
Your words will become creations,
For you are a living God,
Don't let this fact seem odd.

Life Like A Flower

Life like a flower,
Start like a seed,
Love gives the power,
Soul feels freed.

Food, water, light,
Seed builds its roots,
Soul becomes bright,
Spirituality shoots.

Many stuck by Maya,
The truth few cherish,
World burns like fire,
Lucky are those who flourish.

Life like a flower,
End like a seed,
Love gives the power,
Soul becomes freed.

Life Of Deceit

Feeling the love inside,
One is grounded deep,
The soul within cried,
Happiness is what you reap.

Worldly love temporary,
Attachment almost beat,
The True Guru will carry,
Over this life of deceit.

Eating sleeping working,
What good do these bring?
What will you say to The King,
When He will take your ring.

Sustaining life for you,
Will you not lose you in you?
Serve selflessly too,
Your desires will become true.

Worldly love temporary,
Attachment almost beat,
The True Guru will carry,
Over this life of deceit.

Many ways of life persist,
Few find the infinite light,
Actually only one way exists,
Lovingly love The Bright.

Find the company of saints,
Meditate and vibrate,
Experience the soul paints,
Never is it too late.

Worldly love temporary,
Attachment almost beat,
The True Guru will carry,
Over this life of deceit.

Light And Darkness

All that exists, is light and darkness,
Without darkness, how can there be light?
Without day, how can there be night?
All that exists, is light and darkness.

There is no such thing as darkness,
Only lack of light,
There is no night,
Only the end of the day.

There is no such thing as day,
Only lack of darkness,
There is no day,
Only the end of the night.

Such utter confusion,
That even just light and darkness,
Two constants,
Become endless possibilities.

Such utter allusion,
That even just day and night,
Two infinities,
Become endless probabilities.

There is no light,
There is no darkness,
They are just illusions,
Fabricated delusions.

There is only one conclusion,
There is only One,
Just Love.

Like A Gun To The Head

Like a gun to the head,
Trying to breathe,
Panting deeply,
Trying to plead.

There's no escape,
The time has come,
The sun is down,
The mind is torn.

Like a bullet in the brain,
Destroying a perfect shell,
Perfectly made imperfect,
But no one to tell.

They yell,
With no sound,
Voice box is out of order,
The time has come around.

As a foghorn blows in the distance,
The messenger of death arrives,
In his cloak of timeless darkness,
The soul is seized and guilty for time.

Screaming, crying, devastated,
The soul realises the afterlife,
Repenting its sins,
Is sent into the cycle once again.

Life is more precious than the diamond,
But wasted more than the sewage,
What an atrocity, what a shame,
But in the end, who is to blame?

Looking Back

Looking back, life is all planned,
Universe wants us to progress,
So our mind is not dammed,
And our life is not messed.

Looking back, all desires are fulfilled,
Universe grants our wishes,
This law cannot be killed,
It's like water to the fishes.

Looking back, we are not in control,
Universe works everything out,
Realise we're perfect and whole,
So we don't have to run about.

Looking back, the universe loves all,
Universe creates, sustains and destroys,
Universe is our mirror, not our wall,
We are its puppets and toys.

Love Conquers, Kindness Kills

Love conquers the ego,
And kindness kills separation,
Compassion destroys anger,
Charity annihilates greed,
And truth cuts the lies,
And wisdom buries the intellect,
Sweetness shoots rudeness,
Light eats the dark,
And courage burns shallowness,
Intelligence strangles cleverness,
Experience slaps knowledge,
Freedom slits solitude,
And service breaks selfishness.

Love For Each Other

The love of two for each other moves the world,
It travels into the hearts of all uncurled.
Piercing all problems and conflicts, it rides the high bird unfurled,
Such is the power of love, of love.

Perfection exists in this state of bliss,
A time of stillness not to be missed.
Light in the dark, the heart carries you,
Little things in life left, the two so true.

The souls rejoice, they have united once more,
Two become one, the spiritual law.
The individual crawls through their journey,
But together do they grow, the Thou and me.

In joy, in sadness, in conflict, activity,
The comfort in silence a sure sign of clickery.
Create, take and sharing all things,
Realising the oneness, the angels sing.

Two become four and then still more,
Unity, love, self sufficiency universally core.
A utopia? Ideal? Perhaps nothing more,
But a worthwhile aim, love not war.

The love of two for each other moves the world,
It travels into the hearts of all uncurled.
Piercing all problems and conflicts, it rides the high bird unfurled,
Such is the power of love, of love.

Strength in breaking through any layer,
Humanity life's religion, breath it's prayer.
The love of two expanded my free dove,
Such is the power of love, of love.

Loving Everything

He loves the brain,
He loves the sky,
He loves the rain,
And knows how and why.

She loves her enemies,
She loves her house,
She loves her babies,
And even her spouse.

Their actions are good,
Their hearts are pure,
They welcome all through their door,
And God they have understood.

They love all and everything, everywhere,
So why then do they cut their hair?

Loving Hate

Bright dark,
Divine devil,
Invisible mark,
Uneven level.

Pleasuring pain,
Happily sad,
Madly sane,
Good bad.

Ying Yang,
Imbalanced balance,
Silent sang,
Solid valance,

Enjoyed suffering,
Timely late,
Empty stuffing,
Loving hate.

Meditate To Win Win Never Lose

Meditate to win win never lose,
Never need to do the booze,
Less time you want to snooze,
Meditate to win win never lose.

Meditate to win win never lose,
Whatever path you want to use,
Let the inner peace ooze,
Meditate to win win never lose.

Meditate to win win never lose,
May your mind never confuse,
Let the light within infuse,
Meditate to win win never lose.

Meditate to win win never lose,
No need to speak abuse,
Forgive all and excuse,
Meditate to win win never lose.

Meditate to win win never lose,
Concentrate on the sky blues,
Deliberate on the rainbow hues,
Meditate to win win never lose.

Meditate to win win never lose,
Life is a burning fuse,
Death is sending the news,
Meditate to win win never lose.

Meditate to win win never lose,
All hate you must refuse,
Only love you must choose,
Meditate to win win never lose.

No Other Name

I don't need to say any other name, but your name,
Everlasting, All pervading Lord, Forever the same,
I'm forever a sacrifice unto you, I am totally lame,
Everything a blessing from You, no need to blame.

No Words

No words.
Just silence.
Listen.

No words.
Just guidance.
Accept.

No words.
Just love.
Project.

No words.
Just life.
Reflect.

No words.
Just experience.
Experiment.

No words.
Just wisdom.
Share.

No words.
Just being.
Be.

No words.
Just You,
Just You,
Just You,
Alone.

Sat Naam.

Now Is The Time

Now is the time, and the time is now,
Be courageous as a King,
Be the light of everlasting,
The time is now, and now is the time.

Now is the age, and the age is now,
Be glorious as a Queen,
Be the sight of the Unseen,
The age is now, and now is the age.

Now is the place, and the place is now,
Be bright as a star,
Be the guidance to afar,
The place is now, and now is the place.

Now is the space, and the space is now,
Be balanced as a scale,
Be the strength to prevail,
The space is now, and now is the space.

Now is the moment, and the moment is now,
Be rooted as a Tree,
Be the Lotus so free,
The moment is now, and now is the moment.

Now is the time, and the time is now,
Be gracious as a King,
Be the light of everlasting,
The time is now, and now is the time.

Ocean Apart

Your light transmits warm,
Your eyes deep love,
My soul shouts transform,
Fly high pure dove.

Longing to see overdue,
The time dawns to depart,
My soul longs to meet you,
But we sit an ocean apart.

Oh, God Save My Soul

Oh, God can you save my soul,
Oh God, will you show me this life's goal,
Protect me from the evils of the world,
As I have not listened, I have not heard.

Oh God, take me to the heavens and set me free,
Take me where the Truth will be,
Send me across this worldly ocean,
And give me your love and devotion.

I am trapped in this desire,
Without your mercy I cannot respire,
Set me free,
And shine your light on me.

God, I beg for your mercy at your feet,
Give me the power to learn what you teach,
Please emancipate my troubled soul,
And let me do what you have told.

So, God protect me from the evils of the world,
I wish I had listened and heard,
Oh, God, will you show me this life's goal,
And ultimately, save my soul.

On The Outside People Are Pretty

On the outside people are pretty,
But on the inside they are ugly,
On the outside people talk deeply,
But on the inside they are shallow,
On the outside people are tall,
But on the inside they are small,
On the outside people are charming,
But on the inside they are withdrawn,
On the outside people are sweet,
But on the inside they are sour,
On the outside people are loving,
But on the inside they are judging,
On the outside people are open,
But on the inside they are divided,
On the outside people are happy,
But on the inside they are empty.

The inner and outer worlds must be balanced,
In order to achieve authenticity,
The inner and outer worlds must be synchronised,
In order to achieve equanimity.

For the truth creates simplicity,
And simplicity removes the tension,
For the truth creates clarity,
And clarity removes the complication.

Speaking truth, hearing truth, living truth,
Balances the inner and outer realities,
Making it possible to live an extraordinary life,
Free from tension, complication and duality.

Only One Way

There's only one way to light,
To become it,
To drop off the loads,
Which you choose to carry.

There's only one way to marriage,
To marry yourself,
Within yourself,
Giving you your innocence.

There's only one way to God,
To live like a God,
Full of grace, dignity and Divinity,
Bringing you to humility.

There's only one way to heaven,
To bring heaven to earth,
By removing the past karmas,
Which keep you trapped here.

There's only one way to beauty,
To see the beauty in everyone,
All people and all things,
Leaving behind your judgements.

There's only one way to truth,
To speak it and live it,
In all of life's situations,
Being constant and dedicated.

There's only one way to perfection,
To find you're perfect already,
By taking a deep trip within,
Life is lived in the present.

There's only one way to love,
To love unconditionally,
To accept all as they are,
Removing life's duality.

Only one way,
But many roads to there,
Destination is the same,
Paths may be different.

Only one way,
In my opinion,
Your opinion equally valid,
World can work for everyone.

Our Beautiful Soul

Soul, oh beautiful Soul,
Of our mind take control,
Perfection, oh beautiful Perfection,
Become our heart's affection.

Way, oh beautiful Way,
Give us humility to pray,
Path, oh beautiful Path,
Mind needs a cleansing bath.

Beauty, oh beautiful Beauty,
Soul has become our duty,
Lord, oh beautiful Lord,
Serving is our reward.

Light, oh beautiful Light,
You're brighter than the bright,
Star, oh beautiful Star,
Guide us to afar.

Guru, oh beautiful Guru,
Clear our blocks to you,
Divine, oh beautiful Divine,
Your nectar is sublime.

Time, oh beautiful Time,
Stop your ticking chime,
Death, oh beautiful Death,
God be our last life breath.

Path, oh beautiful Path,
Mind needs a cleansing bath.
Way, oh beautiful Way,
Give us humility to pray.

Perfection, oh beautiful Perfection,
Become our heart's affection.
Soul, oh beautiful Soul,
Of our mind take control.

Our Soul Mate

Everyone looking for a soul mate,
Everyone searching everywhere,
Everyone wants to be great,
Everyone searching here and there.

Soul mate is our own soul,
Without which we're incomplete,
Soul is this life's goal,
To be at the Guru's feet.

Sexual desire is out of control,
Anger has taken over all,
Difficult to pay Karma's toll,
Life has started to stall.

Humility is the way out,
Love for God has made me dust,
No more needing to wander about,
Relationship with soul is a must.

I trust it all makes sense,
In the greater scheme of everything,
We forget God at our own expense,
My head to Guru's feet I bring.

Only true love which lasts forever,
Is relationship with the spirit,
Transitory world will not last ever,
To my soul everything I commit.

Peace by Piece

We must create peace,
Peace by piece,
Every part by part,
Every heart by heart.

Let us make a start,
Let peace be the art,
Of creating peace within,
Let us now begin.

Time for war is over,
Time for peace is here,
Of hate let's stand clear,
Let compassion be our spear.

Everything will add up,
Like water filling a cup,
If we change ourselves,
Things will change themselves.

Creating a paradigm shift,
With hope as our catalyst,
Humanity will unite,
Under one banner of light.

Just like the coloured rainbow,
Understands and knows,
It emerges from one light,
One source, one might.

We must unite in humanity,
Leaving behind our insanity,
This vision is not vanity,
It can be our chosen reality.

Your participation is requested,
Your participation is required,
Fill the heart with compassion,
Peace will become a passion.

Let us make a start,
Let peace be the art,
Of creating peace within,
Let us now begin.

We must create peace,
Peace by piece,
Every part by part,
Every heart by heart.

People All Around

People all around,
Spying and prying,
Sighing and lying,
Not knowing or growing, they die.

People all around,
Trying and buying,
Eyeing and spying,
Not growing or knowing, they die.

In a meditative trance,
I enter, to another world,
And take a glance,
Of what has, before me, been unfurled.

Something more than the people,
All around me,
Something more than our surroundings,
My crown has become a steeple.

Such a rare opportunity to see,
What we really are,
Such a chance to be,
One with the brightest star.

Yet still there are,
People all around,
Spying and prying,
Sighing and lying,
Not knowing or growing, they die.

People all around,
Trying and buying,
Eyeing and spying,
Not growing or knowing,
They waste their lives.

Positive Affirmations

Night is completely dark,
Sky is totally torn,
Gone has the spark,
Only dusk without dawn.

Change has now come,
From darkness, to light,
Illuminated like the sun,
From weakness, to might.

Pain has now gone,
From blind, to sight,
Light has now shone,
From dim, to bright.

Mind now the slave,
From wrong, to right,
No more in life's cave,
From black, to white.

Soul now the driver,
From shallow, to height,
Being death's survivor,
From stone, to kite.

Night has forever passed,
Sky is now always bright,
Gone has the past,
Victory in the inner fight.

Purpose Of Life

Purpose of life,
To be fulfilled,
To be immortal,
To be stilled.

Purpose of death,
To end separation,
To end suffering,
To end illusion.

Life's actions weighed,
Is account in profit,
Righteous Judge of Dharma,
Knows accounts in deficit.

Reincarnation the system,
Governs life and death,
Karma the universal law,
Prana the life force breath.

Apana the eliminating energy,
Dharma the universal path,
The way of the householder,
Meditation the cleansing bath.

Love the highest expression,
Truth the highest virtue,
Humility the highest radiance,
Higher still is living Truth.

No need to be confused,
No need to live in fear,
Live dead whilst alive,
God is always here.

Separation with God,
Is the only fear,
The one cost of union,
God is always near.

Life should be fulfilled,
With the perfection of soul,
Connect to soul daily,
So water fills the bowl.

Wave becomes the ocean,
Night becomes the day,
Moon becomes the sun,
For this blessing, I pray.

Purpose of death,
To calculate devotion,
To clarify Truth,
To cease separation.

Purpose of life,
To love fearlessly,
To pray devotedly,
To live happily.

Science Of Love

Yoga a relationship,
Union to infinity,
But do not trip,
Seek only divinity.

Kundalini at the root,
Ida the left feminine,
Sushumna the central route,
Pingala the right masculine.

Pranayama the breath clock,
Asana the body positioning,
Bhanda the body locks,
Mudra the hand conditioning.

Mantra the chant vibration,
Universal language of sound,
Paves the path to liberation,
Creating an effect so profound.

Pineal the soul's seat,
The crown is the home,
Pituitary is incomplete,
Turban the crown's dome.

Tenth gate the doorway,
It takes you to a place,
Before the rise of day,
It brings you to a space.

Becoming humble the key,
Listening to the vibration,
Yoga shall set you free,
Bliss an everlasting sensation.

Meditation becomes the food,
Truthful living the water,
Serving becomes the mood,
No need for any slaughter.

Crown's light is glowing,
Ego's darkness is going,
Source of life is flowing,
Only the love is showing.

Sharing Is Caring

Life not shared,
Is life lost.
Positivism not shared,
Is positivism lost.

Wisdom not shared,
Is wisdom lost.
Experience not shared,
Is experience lost.

Heart not shared,
Is heart lost.
Love not shared,
Is love lost.

Light not shared,
Is karmic cost.
Anything not shared,
Is everything lost.

Sikh-ing

If you want, you will get,
If you ask, you will receive,
If you seek, you will find,
Such is the common law of these Universes.

Learn not to want materialism,
And so in the future,
Or some point in time,
You shall not get greed.

Learn to only ask for the Truth,
And so at one point in time,
Whether it be day or night,
You shall receive the peace of mind.

Such is the common law of these universes,
One can seek,
And by Sikh-ing,
You shall find the Truth,
And forever be in peace.

Sikhism Of Love

Sikhism is an essence,
Sikhism is about awareness,
Sikhism is a defence,
Sikhism is about fairness.

Sikhism is in loving,
Sikhism is about equality,
Sikhism is in knowing,
Sikhism is about creativity.

Sikhism is in purity,
Sikhism is complete,
Sikhism is in security,
Sikhism is elite.

Sikhism is a reality,
Sikhism is about light,
Sikhism is a totality,
Sikhism is about sight.

Sikhism is in being,
Sikhism is about sharing,
Sikhism is in seeing,
Sikhism is about caring.

Sikhism is spirituality,
Sikhism is in progressing,
Sikhism is divinity,
Sikhism is a blessing.

Sikhism is in showing,
Sikhism is about humility,
Sikhism is in growing,
Sikhism is about humanity.

Sikhism is submission,
Sikhism is about uplifting,
Sikhism is ambition,
Sikhism is about leading.

Sikhism is in healing,
Sikhism is a peace,
Sikhism is in feeling,
Sikhism is a release.

Sikhism is in serving,
Sikhism is about soul,
Sikhism is in learning,
Sikhism is about goal.

Sikhism is quality,
Sikhism is about balancing,
Sikhism is immortality,
Sikhism is about embracing.

Sikhism is perfect,
Sikhism is infinity,
Sikhism is respect,
Sikhism is simplicity.

Love is purity, spirituality, healing and perfect.
Love is complete, progressing, peace and infinity.
Love is security, divinity, feeling and respect.
Love is elite, blessing, release and simplicity.

Sikhism is of love,
Love is in everything,
Love gives you joy,
Love is the King.

So Many Lifetimes

Oh my Beloved Lord,
It's been so many lifetimes,
I've been waiting for so long,
Your Vision is my lifeline.

Oh my Beloved Lord,
When will you embrace me?
My heart is in agony,
In separation I'm not free.

So many lifetimes I've wasted,
So many days I've wasted,
So many nights I've wasted,
So many breaths I've wasted.

So many lives without purpose,
So many lives wasted in lust,
So many lives gathering wealth,
So many lives collecting dust.

Now the balance is bust,
The path of God is blessed,
Every moment so precious,
Every moment I request.

Oh my Beloved Lord,
Please keep me at Your Feet,
May I not waste another life,
Until You, Oh Lord, I meet.

Sometimes Life Is Too Much

Sometimes life is too much,
Sometimes life is too less,
Human life is such,
A perfectly organised mess.

So many beautiful people,
So many beautiful creatures,
So many beautiful sounds,
So many beautiful features.

Teachers in everyone,
Answers all within,
Heart and head balanced,
Life we can win.

A never-ending motivation,
To be one with everything,
A never-ending aspiration,
To hear the universe sing.

A perfection beyond perfection,
An experience beyond words,
Falling in love with all,
Hearing the unheard.

Seeing the unseen,
Being at heart's centre,
Heaven is on Earth,
Guru is the mentor.

The bliss so blissful,
The peace so peaceful,
Water filling the cup,
Empty is now full.

Human life is such,
A perfectly organised mess,
Sometimes life is too much,
Sometimes life is too less.

Such A Wondrous Play

What a wondrous play,
Puppets moving obliviously,
Through life and death,
Never knowing the drama's purpose.

Reality seems so real,
Everything in a mysterious coordination,
Everything working and ideal,
Oh, it is such a wondrous play.

With skies of azure, full of reason,
Seas of sapphire, endless and beautiful,
Trees of emerald, changing with season,
Wow, it is such a wondrous play.

To few who realise the deceptive play,
And wake up to see the Truth,
Are forever in peace and find their way,
And they shout, "It's such a wondrous play!"

The puppeteer alone understands the drama's purpose,
Alone knows why, how and when,
Yet even then,
Is forever enjoying this universal theatre,
That is always staging,
Such a wondrous play.

The Answer Infinitely Simple

The answer infinitely simple,
Practice a difficult endeavour,
Falling into the minds deep dimple,
Excuses innumerable and clever.

Waiting for the right time to come,
Growing older and wiser,
Present is the moment sweet one,
Rise up to the commands of the Advisor.

Awaking in the ambrosial hour,
A discipline of sleeping in advance,
Experience the atmospheric power,
Realise the world's playful dance.

Days play out divinely,
Angels serve indiscriminately,
Love from above dripping benignly,
Requests gifted finely.

The answer infinitely simple,
Practice a difficult endeavour,
Rise out of the minds deep dimple,
Experience the blissful forever.

The Bustle Of Life

The hustle of trees,
The bustle of life,
The stormy seas,
The rustle of leaves.

Great Mother Earth,
Honey bees,
Great Coral Reef,
Countless teas.

Boats from ashore,
Rainbows of allure,
Shadows afore,
Skies of azure.

Ever so many,
Items of praise,
How to count,
God's infinite rays.

World is a phase,
Temporary like life,
Life's in a daze,
Cut it with a knife.

Dice is thrown,
Window shown,
Spirituality grown,
On the path home.

Blown out of proportion,
Abortion not the issue,
Our life's in caution,
Body's loosing tissue.

Death is a phase,
Temporary like life,
Prayer clears the daze,
Meditation is the knife.

The Essence Of Life

Join in, join up,
Brand me, make me,

People say, people do,
People act and follow through.

Lose the faith, lose the self,
Lose the essence of life.

Change me, change we,
Dress me, Impress me,

People hear, but do not listen,
People lose the chance to glisten.

Waste the life, waste the time,
Waste the essence of life.

Stand tall, stand out,
Make yourself, make it count,

Simply say, simply do,
Live not the life of me and you.

Live true, live pure,
Live the life worthy of no more.

Respect life, respect all,
Feel the essence of life.

The Eyes Are Drenched

The eyes are drenched,
With love of Infinity,
The ears are attuned,
To words of Divinity.

Mysteries of the trinity,
The mind understands,
The heart knows of,
All seas and lands.

Like the joining of hands,
Devotee joins the Lord,
Inner battle is won,
Shabad is the sword.

Immortal nectar being poured,
Into the heart centre,
Projecting love into the world,
Calms the wild temper.

This is a life venture,
Healing people and Earth,
Mother Earth so loving,
Being abused since birth.

What is joy worth?
What is life's price?
Why is happiness impermanent?
Why is love like dice?

Devotees live a joyous life,
All carefree and unlimited,
Devotees find life priceless,
They keep life simplified.

Devotees lives are dignified,
They only choose God's love,
Devotees see God in everyone,
Suffering they rise above.

Devotees become the dove,
Moving in God's will,
Love of God is permanent,
Mind is now still.

Climbing life's hill,
Peace is obtained,
Be willing to grow,
Peace has sustained.

Body no longer drained,
Heart is always protected,
Union has been achieved,
Mind is now concentrated.

The ears are attuned,
To words of Divinity,
The eyes are drenched,
With love of Infinity.

The Five Beloveds Of The Khalsa

The five beloveds of the Khalsa,
The five are purity personified,
The five have no gender,
The five are purity glorified.

The five beloveds of the Khalsa,
The five are purity beautified,
The five have no contender,
The five are purity simplified.

The five control the five thieves,
Lust, greed, anger, attachment, ego,
The five turn seeds into trees,
They let the Naam inside flow.

The five contain the five virtues,
Love, truth, compassion, contentment, humility,
The five only speak what is True,
They drink the Nectar of immortality.

The five traverse the five realms,
Righteousness, wisdom, humility, action, truth,
The five turn a stem into Elm,
They glow with the vitality of youth.

The five personify the five beloveds,
Kindness, righteousness, order, courage, leadership,
The five's egos have been beheaded,
Their mouths have become Guru's lips.

The five vibrate the five vibrations,
S, T, N, M, A from Satnaam,
The five stay in Godly sensations,
They remain conscious and calm.

The five recite the five prayers,
Jap, Jaap, Swaiye, Chopai, Anand,
The five stay radiant and aware,
They echo the Guru's command.

The five possess the five articles,
Underwear, bracelet, sword, comb, hair,
The five recite Vaheguru with each particle,
They remained righteous and fair.

The five dictate the five senses,
Sight, taste, touch, hearing, smell,
The five are God's army defences,
In purity do their hearts dwell.

The five exceed the five elements,
Air, earth, fire, water, ether,
The five leave a sweet scent,
They remain absorbed in prayer.

The five surpass the five matters,
Gas, solid, plasma, liquid, space,
The five cannot be shattered,
They live in humility and grace.

The five are purity simplified,
The five have no contender,
The five are purity beautified,
The five beloveds of the Khalsa.

The five are purity glorified,
The five have no gender,
The five are purity personified,
The five beloveds of the Khalsa.

The Fly

Once I saw a fly,
Very small and fast,
Buzzing its way around the room,
In search of an exit.

What a foolish fly,
Didn't know all the windows were closed,
Didn't know the art of transparency,
But kept on buzzing in search of an exit.

It traveled from wall to wall,
Again and again, back and forth,
As if to opposite sides of the earth,
All in search of an exit.

I don't know what happened to the fly,
But it gave me realization of life,
Of life as we don't yet know it,
That we are all in search of the same exit.

We wander endlessly to find the exit,
From pole to pole, from universe to universe,
Only to find the exit is not outside,
But rather inside us,
Waiting to be discovered and opened.

This is the exit to everlasting happiness, bliss,
Contentment, joy, poise and peace of mind,
Such an exit is very precious yet hidden well,
It is too important to not be searched for,
Remember this whenever you see a fly buzzing.

The Game of Love

You indulge in pleasure,
And study to be clever,
Unaware before a shove,
You play the game of love.

Be careful oh mortal,
This life leads to one portal,
With the right hand,
One could become grand.

You indulge in pleasure,
And study to be clever,
Unaware before a shove,
You play the game of love.

The five traps are wise,
They learn to disguise,
The infinity of the Lord,
Distrust, unassured.

You indulge in pleasure,
And study to be clever,
Unaware before a shove,
You play the game of love.

Love can be irrational,
Without it life is dull,
Whatever happens oh sibling,
Remain blissful and sing.

Life a gifted glove,
Don't throw it in the bin
You play the game of love,
Only play to win.

The Journey Of Love

There's a fire in my heart,
Night and Day,
I'm on the journey at the start,
With love guiding my way.

Truth, peace and perfection,
Surrounds me in every part,
I've been given the direction,
Being guided by my heart.

The feeling so surreal,
In mind, body and soul,
A feeling so warm and real,
Helping fulfil this life's goal.

Never wanting to let the love go,
Willing to give everything away,
Never wishing to stop the heart's flow,
Willing to make that love stay.

Like so perfect a painting of art,
Shining beauty all around,
Spreading love to my heart,
Like so perfect a melody of sound.

With love guiding my way,
Ending the journey from the start,
Night and Day,
There's a fire in my heart.

The Light Of My Life

The light of my life is the Guru,
The Guru is the light of my life,
The Shabad is the light of my soul,
The light of my soul is the Shabad.

Without You, Oh True Guru,
Where would I be?
Oh True Guru, Without You,
How could I see?

When I didn't even know it,
You guided my life,
You guided my life,
When I didn't even know it.

What can I possibly give to You,
Give to the Great Giver?
To You what can I possibly give,
Than my mind, body and soul.

How can words express my love,
My love for the Guru,
My love for the Guru,
How can words express my love.

The Shabad is the light of my soul,
The light of my soul is the Shabad,
The Guru is the light of my life,
The light of my life is the Guru.

The Lord Is

The Lord is kind in so many ways,
The Lord is perfect in so many ways,
The Lord is beautiful in so many ways,
The Lord is creative in so many ways.

The Lord is merciful in so many ways,
The Lord is forgiving in so many ways,
The Lord is giving in so many ways,
The Lord is graceful in so many ways.

The Lord is immortal. The Lord is infinite.
The Lord is all joy. The Lord is all powerful.
How to know the end of the Endless?
Who to place hopes in but the Lord?

No one can know the end of the Endless.
Place hopes in no one but the Lord.
Why go to anyone else? Everything created will die.
The Lord is within, yet without.

Search deep within. Listen deep within.
Make negative thoughts positive through Mantra.
Let the thoughts flow in and flow out.
Listen deep within. Follow deep within.

Answer always there. Prayer always heard.
Answer comes in form of Saints and environments.
Answer comes in form of signs and space.
Prayer always heard. Careful what you ask.

The Lord is wondrous in so many ways,
The Lord is colourful in so many ways,
The Lord is guiding in so many ways,
The Lord is showing in so many ways.

The Lord is carefree in so many ways,
The Lord is creating in so many ways,
The Lord is sustaining in so many ways,
The Lord is destroying in so many ways.

The Moment of Love

When? What day?
What time? What moment?
When will you come and meet me Oh Lord?
The agony. The separation.
The pain is too much to bear.

What must I do before you grant me a blessed moment of Your
love?
I await Your Grace, Oh Almighty giver of life.
The pleasures of the world have become tasteless and insipid.
Every moment I forget you is a moment of endless pain.
I submit. I submit. I submit. Forever.

I'm lost. Which way should I turn to take me to my true home?
Who will understand my pain?
Great giver of everything, show me Your mercy.
I'm an egomaniac and have no motivation to practice the
Teachings.
I search. I search. I search. For Your light and love.

Why do you worry my child?
Don't you think it will all be taken care of?
The servant is blessed when the time is right.
Your job is to keep trying.

Do not fear. Do not have enmity.
Walk with grace. Be at your center.
Search your heart everyday.
That moment when you remember me, is a graceful moment.

The Pain Of Separation

The pain of separation,
A part of me missing,
A deep desperation,
My soul is reminiscing.

I've lost my foundation,
Forgot the destination,
Body flowing with temptation,
The world's my salvation.

Started doing meditation,
Giving the mind relaxation,
I've been given realisation,
The world's an animation.

It's time for concentration,
Fill the heart with admiration,
Light gives me fascination,
Feeling the love's vibration.

No need for conversation,
There's no more hesitation,
Gone has the isolation,
It's time for transformation.

The jewel of life too short,
Breath's wearing out creation,
Each moment Karma's court,
Coming near my cremation.

My soul's in elevation,
Such a deep integration,
I've found the destination,
No more pain of separation.

The Purity Of Khalsa

Khalsa is the Purity,
Purity is the Word,
Purity is the Guru,
Purity is seen and heard.

Khalsa has no gender,
Khalsa has no creed,
Khalsa has no contender,
Khalsa has no greed.

Khalsa has no dye,
Khalsa has no caste,
Khalsa has no lie,
Khalsa has no contrast.

Khalsa has no persecution,
Khalsa has no injustice,
Khalsa has no discrimination,
Khalsa has no artifice.

Khalsa has no apprehension,
Khalsa has no revulsion,
Khalsa has no tension,
Khalsa has no compulsion.

Khalsa has total equality,
Khalsa has total fairness,
Khalsa has total dignity,
Khalsa has total awareness.

Khalsa has total honesty,
Khalsa has total radiance,
Khalsa has total integrity,
Khalsa has total acceptance.

Khalsa has total infinity,
Khalsa has total liberation,
Khalsa has total creativity,
Khalsa has total dedication.

Khalsa has total stability,
Khalsa has total validity,
Khalsa has total tranquillity,
Khalsa has total humility.

Purity is the Guru,
Purity is the Word,
Khalsa is the Purity,
Purity is seen and heard.

The Self Discipline Song

No more will random events dominate,
I will keep to my word,
No more will I let others down,
I will seek to be seen and heard.

My actions will be true,
My heart will be pure,
My conduct will be good,
My body will be as it should.

Life is a responsibility,
Which I agree to take,
I shall keep fit and healthy,
And finish what I make.

Self discipline is what I seek,
To do what I want to do,
To always follow through,
With my actions being true.

No more will random events dominate,
I will keep to my word,
No more will I let others down,
I will seek to be seen and heard.

The Sound Of Infinity

The day has come,
The sky is clear,
The darkness has gone,
The Guru is near.

The world is torn,
The confusion is here,
The emptiness is born,
The creation's in fear.

What shall I do?
How will we cope?
Where's the way out?
Where's the freedom rope?

Meditating consciously,
Contemplating repeatedly,
Concentrating fearlessly,
On the sound of Infinity.

No more duality,
No more confusion,
No more darkness,
No more delusion.

The day has come,
The sky is clear,
The darkness has gone,
The Guru is near.

The Source Of Love

Oh God, if I could attain You by bowing my head,
I would bow countless times in all the four directions.
Oh God, if I could attain You by reciting the Gurmantar,
I would recite Vaheguru until my tongue recites it automatically.
Oh God, if I could attain You by meditating on You,
I would sit in meditation at the Third Eye night and day.
Oh God, if I could attain You by gazing the universe,
I would inspect every particle of it and commit it to memory.
Oh God, if I could attain You by serving,
I would serve all your creation a million times over.
Oh God, if I could attain You by controlling my breath,
I would inhale, exhale and suspend the breath constantly.
Oh God, if I could attain You by doing your Kirtan,
I would sing out aloud in all the Ragas of the universe.
Oh God, if I could attain You by practicing yogic postures,
I would sit in them perfectly throughout the four ages.
Oh God, You can be attained in so many ways,
But without love for You, what use are any of them?
Oh God, separation from You is my only fear,
I would do anything to avoid it.

By bowing my head in utter humility,
By reciting Gurbani and applying it to my life,
By meditating on God's greatness and virtues,
By adoring God's perfection through God's creation,
By serving God's creation selflessly without reward,
By breathing each and every breath consciously,
By singing the praises of the Wondrous God,
By practicing Yogic postures with love,
The All-Loving God has become my only support.
What greater love is there than the Source of Love?
What more permanent love is there than the Imperishable God?
By Guru's Grace, I have obtained this limited understanding.

The Wonderful Creator

Glorious. Transcendent.
Flawless. Immanent.
Perfect. Illustrious.
Magnificent. Fearless.

Immortal. Kindest.
Beautiful. Undying.
Unborn. Brightest.
Enlightened. Calming.

Most grand. Most loving.
Most giving. Most vast.
Highest. Most glorious.
Brightest. Most pious.

Most beautiful. Most kind.
Most tender. Most wonderful.
Entwined. Most pure.
Aligned. Most secure.

Without enemy. Without lies.
All Truth. Without envy.
Without desire. Without need.
All love. Without greed.

Without hate. Without ego.
All light. Without fate.
Without death. Without life.
All knowing. Without strife.

Without caste. Without gender.
All powerful. Without haste.
Without lust. Without anger.
All glowing. Without hunger.

Without name. Without attachment.
All bright. Without blame.
Without insecurity. Without pain.
All immortal. Without strain.

The Word Of All Word

Never will you look back again,
From suffering, attachment and pain,
Shri Guru Granth Sahib Ji,
Will set your entire being free.

Written in poetry,
It relates you to Infinity.
Written in song,
Has vibrations like the Gong.

Written in vibration,
An everlasting sensation.
Written in mood,
It's our daily drink and food.

Written in flow,
There's no break in the glow.
Written in light,
It's brighter than the bright.

Written in humility,
It brings you to tranquillity.
Written by the Masters,
Avoids the authenticity disaster.

Written in heart,
There's no greater work of art.
Written in joy,
All egos it shall destroy.

Written in words,
It's the Word of all word.
Written in love,
It shall elevate us high above.

Shri Guru Granth Sahib Ji,
Will set your entire being free,
From suffering, attachment and pain,
Never will you look back again.

There Is A Light In My Heart

There is but a light in the sky,
Which ignites my heart,
A light brighter than the sun,
Two have become one.

There is a light in the ethers,
It sees everyone,
It judges no one,
There is a light in my heart.

There is a power in my heart,
Stronger than strength itself,
More beautiful than beauty,
There is a light in my heart.

There is an art in my heart,
Forever dancing to the Earth,
Like the start has become the finish,
There is a light in my heart.

There is a beauty in my heart,
More vast than vastness,
Life is my duty,
There is a light in my heart.

There is a diamond in my heart,
More precious than precious,
A life of devotion,
There is a light in my heart.

There is a stillness in my heart,
A constant connection,
To the Divine within,
There is a light in my heart.

There is a light in the ethers,
It sees everyone,
It judges no one,
There is a light in my heart.

There is but a light in the sky,
Which ignites my heart,
A light brighter than the sun,
Two have become one.

There She Saws Through The Ether

There she saws through the ether,
Wings spread high, all wish to meet her,
Effortlessly showcasing her flying freedom,
In tune she sings, humi hum hum.

What is to be the future of me? What is my destiny?
Why has the mother allowed me to see, to feel, to hear utter
infestory?
When will the darkness fall? When will it end?
How does the world appear so sublime from so high ahead?
The questions infinitely clever but there she sings, I am God, I am
forever.

A divine dichotomy of contradiction she sees,
Philosophy, science, knowledge goes on as the keys,
Love and fear together play and tease,
Cause, effect, time and space the mighty trance,
She laughs at the drama, life's divine dance.

Slicing the air with her slender wings, she sets her sights, the descent
begins,
The heart's desire to change the world, an energetic alchemy,
baby is born.
Wailing in wonderment promises abundant,
The journey for life's lessons a maze, the absolute made redundant.
The game of life, spin the wheel, is it chance, luck, perhaps Kal's
hunt?

What is thought is made, she screams listen,
The mind rules holding the reigns, the soul follows the creation.
In fun, the moment, the now exists only, The play plays to reach the
final destination,
She screams listen but is not heard, the minds exhilaration, a never
ending end...

In the seven year cycle the body matures, yearning to sour once again, leave she shall,
There she flies higher and higher, altitude not latitude the pull...AKAL!
The myriad of possibilities, the indescribable forever,
Cause, effect, being in the ever, the choice of now, never never.
Never ever never forever and ever, one IS, together IS, forever IS ever.

There she saws through the ether,
Wings spread high, all wish to meet her,
Effortlessly showcasing her flying freedom,
In tune she sings, humi hum hum.

Tree Of Knowledge

Observing the tree,
All fear shall depart,
Desire to be free,
Centred in the heart.

Roots so deeply rooted,
Nothing can effect,
If even all water's looted,
Tree remains perfect.

Trunks stand tall,
Fearlessly they protect,
Shade they serve all,
Nature they respect.

Branches are the lotus,
Kindness they project,
When will we notice,
Tree stays connect.

Leaves always green,
Humility they reflect,
By listening remain serene,
Acting always correct.

Light they need to grow,
Materialism they reject,
Nectar inside is in flow,
Good karma they collect.

Tree is always serving,
Tree is always growing,
Tree is always flowing,
Tree is always glowing.

Tree contains the universe,
Universe contains the tree,
Examine the beauty of creation,
Creator shall set you free.

True Beauty

I see beauty all around,
All around,
I hear the sounds,
Of True Beauty.

Trees of the finest emerald,
Seas of the richest azure,
I hear the sounds,
I see beauty all around.

It's my duty,
To find the source of the sound,
Sometimes I feel down,
Sometimes I have to frown.

True Beauty is as far as the sun,
Once the addiction has begun,
It feels like you've won,
And the goal of life is done.

Universe Takes Care of All

Universe takes care of all,
So why worry my friend?
A reply to every call,
A rule you cannot bend.

A lesson every moment,
The present is precious,
Breath is being spent,
Life can be vicious.

Life can be blissful,
Listening is the key,
Sound current so graceful,
One can simply be.

No judgment in the eyes,
The 'I' is no longer,
No good, nor evil, nor lies,
Aura has grown stronger.

Mantra in the breath,
Only 'Thou' exists,
Whilst alive, accepting death,
Peace can now persist.

Sacrificing to Infinity,
Mind, body and soul,
Now nothing an impossibility,
Love has filled the hole.

Nothing else shall liberate,
Just submission in humility,
Blocks this shall eliminate,
Through love of Divinity.

A rule you cannot bend,
A reply to every call,
So why worry my friend?
Universe takes care of all.

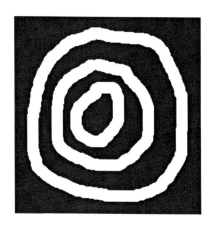

Wahe, Wahe, Wahe Guru

Wahe, Wahe, Wahe Guru,
Jack of all trades,
Master of all,
Magnificent and elusive,
This is what You are My Lord.

Wahe, Wahe, Wahe Guru,
Idiotic, foolish and poor,
Thankful, grateful, small,
Open hearted, undisciplined,
This is what I am My Lord.

Wahe, Wahe, Wahe Guru,
Emperor of emperors,
Queen of Queens,
Everything yet nothing,
This is what You are My Lord.

Wahe, Wahe, Wahe Guru,
Confused, fearful and uncontrolled,
Sharing, caring, great,
Light hearted, innocent,
This what I am My Lord.

When will this bridge between You and me become abridged?
When the time is right.

When will my soul merge with Your Soul?
When you become light.

When will my heart merge with Your Heart?
When you find me in your heart.

When will my mind become my slave and me its master?
When I give you my grace.

In the end it shall be alright,
God shall work it out,
God is the creator, preserver and destroyer,
We are in God's hands as much as God is in our hands,
This co-relationship cannot be falsified,
For it is the Truth everlasting.

What Is Truth?

A question with origins,
From the origin of time,
What is Truth?
And what isn't Truth?

I see people bowing their head,
To their doctrines,
I see people bowing their head,
To their religious leaders.

Doctrines that have been changed,
Are more of man than of Truth,
Called holy and sacred,
Are blindly followed without liberalness.

Religious leaders,
Leading people into war,
Leading people into corruption,
Is this being religious?

The Truth is so cleverly hidden,
The outer eyes are open,
But the inner eyes remain closed.

Truth is the Naam,
Truth is serving the creation,
Truth is loving the creation,
Truth is being True to your True self.

Truth isn't unjustified war,
Truth isn't materialism,
Truth isn't corruption,
Truth isn't intentional lies.

Only the individual can find the Truth,
Individually by seeking
Truth, it is found,
Truth is all around.

Save yourself, whilst you still can.
Be a seeker of Truth.

Wherever You Want Me

My Lord, wherever you want me to go,
I'll go.
My Lord, whenever you want me to die,
I'll die.
My Lord, whenever you want me to live,
I'll live.

My Lord, however big the mountain you give me,
I'll climb.
My Lord, whatever you want me to sacrifice,
I'll sacrifice.
My Lord, whatever order you give me,
I'll obey.

My Lord, Your infinite beauty mesmerises me,
My Lord, Your fearlessness, creativity and love encapsulates me,
My Lord, Your grace, endlessness and perfection fascinates me,
I'm forever at the feet of the Lord of the Universe.

Whispers

Whispers. Even in the darkest corners of existence, one can hear. Sounds of the most terrifying. Sounds of the most extravagant. Sounds of nothingness, drowned by whispers. Whispers. Some of fortune, others of failure. Some of merit, others of demerit. Whispers everywhere, whispers heard but not seen. Whispers, even in the brightest part of the sun, one can hear whispers.

Who Am I?

I possess a cosmos of great,
A world of conjecturable worldly pleasures,
And a universe of never ending,
Light, yet also dark is contained in the palm of my hands,
Time ticks away but I never change.

Who am I?

I have not a physical face seen to man or woman and never will
have,
Beyond the senses of five am I, but in the sixth you can acquire my
power.

Who am I?

To destroy is never me but love is what I see,
I have endless capabilities, to command the three stages of life,
I am of course the almighty Generator, Operator and the Destroyer
of all you see.

Follow me,
Believe in me,
Trust in me,
And I shall set you free.

Why is Life Such a Tornado?

We see the tornado,
Big and fast,
Spinning on its axis,
Destroying all in its path.

We see the human,
Small and sly,
Trying to change the world,
And living a lie.

Everyone thinks everyone's OK,
But everyone is in a battle,
Of the mind, body and soul,
Just as confused as cattle.

So why is life such a tornado?
Because we are mini-tornadoes,
Destroying our own planet,
To have a better quality of life.

Yet all is not lost,
There is still a way out,
By destroying the tornado,
Just don't doubt,
The home can be restored
Forever,
And the Lotus can sprout.

Wonders That Lie In The Beyond

There are wonders that lie in the beyond,
More vast than the ears and eyes that see,
More remote than the remoteness of a thousand acres,
More real than the reality we seldom perceive.

For the arts of the inner world have remained mystery,
For a thousand years, 'til the Sun rose,
And we shall remember the thousands dead,
Who gave their lives so we may live instead.

The power within has not known its peak,
For age and age, after it all began,
But now has come the time to shine,
Brighter than a thousand suns and stars.

For light and light makes life lighter,
Eliminating darkness till beyond the beyond,
So should I seek a thousand worlds,
Or look inside to uncover the pearl.

As there are wonders that lie in the beyond,
More vast than the ears and eyes that see,
More remote than the remoteness of a thousand acres,
More real than the reality we seldom perceive.

Wow Wow Wonderful Vaheguru

Wow, Wow, Wonderful Vaheguru,
You've organised all my affairs,
Wow, Wow, Wonderful Vaheguru,
Now I have no worries or cares.

Wow, Wow, Wonderful Vaheguru,
I live for neither heaven or earth,
Wow, Wow, Wonderful Vaheguru,
You alone are my honour and worth.

Wow, Wow, Wonderful Vaheguru,
You are so many things,
Wow, Wow, Wonderful Vaheguru,
And yet I am nothing.

Wow, Wow, Wonderful Vaheguru,
You are so unlimited,
Wow, Wow, Wonderful Vaheguru,
And yet I'm so limited.

Wow, Wow, Wonderful Vaheguru,
You never die or age,
Wow, Wow, Wonderful Vaheguru,
You save me from my rage.

Wow, Wow, Wonderful Vaheguru,
You're creations are so intricate,
Wow, Wow, Wonderful Vaheguru,
Great ruler of destiny and fate.

Wow, Wow, Wonderful Vaheguru,
My Everlasting King Almighty,
Wow, Wow, Wonderful Vaheguru,
May my heart always sing your praises.

Wow, Wow, Wonderful Vaheguru,
You enjoined me into your service,
Wow, Wow, Wonderful Vaheguru,
I'm enraptured by your perfection.

Your Name

The day whispers,
Your Name.
The night whispers,
Your fame.

The world's become,
So lame.
Our mind must,
Be tamed.

Polluted and stained,
For so long,
When will we understand,
What went wrong.

Let's stay strong,
There's still hope,
Not too late,
To cut the rope.

Remember always,
Never forget,
Source of life,
Our destiny set.

Giver of life,
In all places,
Bringer of death,
Of all spaces.

It's no race,
Just a choice,
Go at your pace,
Heart's your voice.

Noise is going,
Peace inside,
Love is growing,
No more pride.

Face is glowing,
No hate,
Everything's clear,
Perfect state.

Saint and soldier,
No fear,
Radiance of Guru,
Guru's here.

No more tears,
No worldly trait,
Follow the Guru,
Not fate.

Everyone's great,
Soul so pure,
At tenth gate,
Guru's door.

Everyone so sure,
People dying,
Illness everywhere,
People crying.

Maya is lying,
God knows,
Maya is deceiving,
Guru shows.

No more low,
Gurmukh in bliss,
Never stop trying,
Guru insists.

Spreading the light,
Developing soul,
Light so bright,
Complete life's goal.

Our mind must,
Be tamed.
The world's become,
So lame.

The night whispers,
Your fame.
The day whispers,
Your Name.

Author Profiles

Jasdeep Hari Bhajan Singh Khalsa
I am the youngest of four siblings, and a first generation British Sikh born in the United Kingdom, my parents were from India. Going into a public school there were many challenges to my identity, not from the outside from other people, but instead from inside myself. Also, looking back on my life, God and Guru has guided me through every situation of life even though I was unaware of it at the time. I have always had this subtle connection to the spiritual masters and it's through these inner challenges to discover myself and this connection to God and Guru that I've written most of my poetry.

The first poem I wrote when I was just 13 years of age, I am now 21 years of age and still writing. It has been a very interesting spiritual path for me so far and most of my spiritual progression has come through the regular practice of Kundalini Yoga, reading the five Sikh daily meditations called the Nitnem, regularly sitting in meditation and prayer, having conversations with God, meeting spiritual masters, listening to the sound of the Gong and going on a personal development course from Landmark Education.

Onkardeep Singh Khalsa
Hi, I'm Onkardeep, I'm 22 and have been creating art and poems since I was a child. In the big scheme of things my life is a very simple one and one which I have very much enjoyed experiencing. I'm extremely grateful for all the opportunities I have been given, especially those which have allowed me to serve others; this book being one of them.

Every year I look back at myself and I'm astounded at what I have achieved and how far I have progressed. This progression has been down to many factors but in particular it has been my gradual increase in openness to see things from different points of view. To understand, stand-under. Understanding life all depends on how you look at it, and I hope that I can continue to broaden my viewpoints whilst maintaining a focus on my chosen path; the Sikh way of life. 'Life is the journey, no matter the end,
The end is guaranteed, my divine friend' - *Page: 20 - Daily Meditation*

Lightning Source UK Ltd.
Milton Keynes UK
09 December 2009

147303UK00001B/26/P